A PATTERN FOR LIFE

Selected Writings of
Thomas à Kempis

Upper Room Spiritual Classics — Series 2

Selected, edited, and introduced by
Keith Beasley-Topliffe

UPPER ROOM BOOKS

Upper Room Web address: http://www.upperroom.org

Scripture quotations are from the New Revised Standard Version of the Bible, © 1989 by the Division of Christian Education of the National Council of Churches of Christ in the USA. Used by permission. All rights reserved.

The printed decorated paper on the cover is a facsimile reproduction of the original taken from the Catalogue of Decorated Papers produced by the printing works Remondini in Bassano del Grappa, Venice, XVII-XVIII century.

While every effort has been made to secure permission from the rightful copyright holder, we apologize for any inadvertent oversight or error.

Art direction: Michele Wetherbee
Interior design and layout: Nancy Cole

First Printing: October 1998

Library of Congress Cataloging-in-Publication Data

Thomas, à Kempis, 1380–1471.
    A Pattern for Life: selected writings of Thomas à Kempis.
        p.   cm. — (Upper Room spiritual classics. Series 2)
    ISBN 0-8358-0835-1
    1. Meditations. I. Title. II. Series.
BV4821.T47   1998
242—dc21   97-33488
                                                                        CIP

Printed in the United States of America

TABLE OF CONTENTS

INTRODUCTION

The Imitation of Christ, by Thomas à Kempis, has had more influence on Christian spirituality today than any other book except the Bible. From the time of its first appearance around 1420, it has been a best-seller. It was one of the first books to be printed and went through fifty editions before 1500. Even persons who have never read it have received its message through others who have read it, both Catholic and Protestant. Luther, Calvin, and Wesley all cherished it. Its echoes sound in countless hymns.

Despite this popularity, modern readers may find *The Imitation* troubling. Language about despising the world and having contempt for oneself may seem to contradict modern emphases on appreciation of all creation and on self-actualization. But Thomas is talking about a love for Christ so all-consuming that every other love must wither away. If Christ is everything, then all else must be nothing unless it is in Christ or loved for Christ's sake. If the goal is to love God with all one's heart, soul, mind, and strength, then no other goal—personal, communal, or national—can be allowed to stand in the way. And so, says Thomas, one's own will must be put to death so that God's will may be done.

One of the first books published by John Wesley was his own abridged translation of *The Imitation*, which he called *The Christian's Pattern* In the preface he says that it "is impossible for anyone to know the usefulness of this treatise" who has not for one short trip to attend his dying brother (John had gone on to found another monastery), he lived in that community for seventy-two years.

Thomas's primary work within the community was as a copyist. He produced two complete copies of the Bible (ten volumes each) as well as numerous psalters and prayer books. He also served as subprior of the monastery and as novice master. It might have been the latter work, training new members of the community, that inspired him to write out the basic advice on the Christian life that became *The Imitation of Christ.* Certainly the books of *The Imitation* summarize the New Devotion, with many echoes of the preaching and writing of Geert Grote and his early followers.

The four books of *The Imitation* were produced separately and circulated anonymously. This led to many different guesses as to the author's identity. The oldest existing copy of Book I is dated 1424. The oldest manuscript with all four is from 1427. Other early manuscripts contained two or three of the books in various orders and combinations. In 1441, Thomas himself copied out a revised edition, together with some of his sermons and other writings. Thomas also wrote biographies of Geert Grote and other early leaders of the New Devotion.

Thomas died July 25, 1471, in his ninety-second year.

fURThER READING

There are a great many modern English translations of *The Imitation of Christ*, most fairly literal. William C. Creasy has attempted a "re-creation" for modern readers, using reader-response theory to produce a dynamic equivalent paraphrase. Other works by Thomas are not readily available.

Selections from the writings of Geert Grote and other early members of the New Devotion have been collected and translated by John Van Engen in *Devotio Moderna—Basic Writings* (Paulist Press). Some of the writings of Geert's mentor, John of Ruusbroec (1293–1381), are also available from Paulist Press, as are works by Nicholas of Cusa, a contemporary of Thomas who also studied with the Brothers of the Common Life.

NOTE ON The TEXT

The basis for these selections is a 1940 translation by Aloysius Croft and Harold Bolton, originally published by the Bruce Publishing Company. The text has been compared with other modern translations in the process of editing it for length, clarity, and inclusive language. Where possible, scriptural quotations and allusions have been conformed to the language of the New Revised Standard Version (indicated by *italics* in the text). Chapter titles are not those of Thomas but have been created for this volume.

IMITATING CHRIST

From Book I, Chapters 1 and 2

The first book of The Imitation *is a treatise on what it means to live a Christian life. The title of the whole work is from the title Thomas gave to the first chapter: "On the Imitation of Christ."*

"Whoever follows me will never walk in darkness," says the Lord. By these words Christ advises us to imitate his life and habits if we wish to be truly enlightened and free from all blindness of heart. Let our primary effort, therefore, be to study the life of Jesus Christ.

The teaching of Christ is more excellent than all the advice of the saints. Whoever has his spirit will find in it a hidden manna. Now, there are many who hear the gospel often but care little for it because they do not have the spirit of Christ. Yet those who wish to understand fully the words of Christ must try to pattern their whole lives on that of Christ.

What good does it do to speak learnedly about the Trinity if, lacking humility, you displease the Trinity? Indeed it is not learning that makes people holy and just. A virtuous life makes them pleasing to God. I would rather feel contrition than know how to define it. For what would it profit us to know the whole Bible by heart and the principles of all the philosophers if we live without grace and the love of

God? *Vanity of vanities, all is vanity,* except to love God and serve God alone.

This is the greatest wisdom—to seek the kingdom of heaven through contempt of the world. It is vanity, therefore, to seek and trust in riches that perish. It is vanity also to court honor and to be puffed up with pride. It is vanity to follow the lusts of the body and to desire things for which severe punishment must come later. It is vanity to wish for long life and to care little about a well-spent life. It is vanity to be concerned with the present only and not to make provision for things to come. It is vanity to love what passes quickly and not to look ahead where eternal joy abides.

Often recall the proverb: "The eye is not satisfied with seeing, or the ear filled with hearing." Try, moreover, to turn your heart from the love of visible things and bring yourself to invisible things. For those who follow their own evil passions stain their consciences and lose the grace of God.

Everyone naturally desires knowledge. But what good is knowledge without fear of God? Indeed humble peasants who serve God are better than proud intellectuals who neglect their souls to study the course of the stars. Those who know themselves well become little in their own eyes and are not happy when praised by others.

If I knew all things in the world and had not love, what would it profit me before God who will judge me by my deeds?

Shun too great a desire for knowledge, for there is much fretting and delusion in it. Intellectuals like to appear learned and to be called wise. Yet there are many things the knowledge of which does little or no good to the soul, and those who concern themselves about other things than those that lead to salvation are very unwise.

Many words do not satisfy the soul; but a good life eases the mind and a clean conscience inspires great trust in God.

The more you know and the better you understand, the more severely will you be judged, unless your life is also the more holy. Do not be proud, therefore, because of your learning or skill. Rather, fear because of the talent given you. If you think you know many things and understand them well enough, realize at the same time that there is much you do not know. Do not pretend to wisdom, but admit your ignorance. Why prefer yourself to anyone else when many are more learned and more cultured than you?

If you wish to learn and appreciate something worthwhile, love to be unknown and considered as nothing. Truly to know and despise oneself is the best and most perfect counsel. To think of oneself as nothing, and always to think well and highly of others, is the best and most perfect wisdom. So if you see another sin openly or commit a serious crime, do not consider yourself better, for you do not know how long you can remain good. All people are frail, but you must admit that none is more frail than yourself.

UPROOTING EVIL HABITS

From Book I, Chapters 11 and 12

We would enjoy greater peace if we did not concern ourselves with what others say and do. These are no concern of ours. How can someone who meddles in the affairs of others, who seeks strange distractions, and who is little or seldom inwardly recollected, live long in peace?

Blessed are the simple of heart for they shall enjoy peace in abundance.

Why were some of the saints so perfect and so given to contemplation? Because they tried to put to death in themselves all earthly desires. So they could attach themselves to God with all their hearts and freely concentrate their innermost thoughts.

We are too occupied with our own whims and fancies, too taken up with passing things. Rarely do we completely conquer even one vice. We are not inflamed with the desire to improve ourselves day by day and so remain cold and indifferent. If we mortified our bodies perfectly and allowed no distractions to enter our minds, we could appreciate divine things and experience something of heavenly contemplation.

The greatest obstacle, indeed, the only obstacle, is that we are not free from passions and lusts, that we do not try to follow the perfect way of the saints. So when we encounter some slight difficulty, we are too easily dejected and turn to human consolations. If we tried, however, to stand bravely in battle, the help of the Lord from heaven would surely sustain us. For God, who gives us the opportunity of fighting for victory, is ready to help those who carry on and trust in God's grace.

If we let our progress in religious life depend on the observance of its externals alone, our devotion will quickly come to an end. Let us, then, lay the ax to the root that we may be freed from our passions and thus have peace of mind.

If we were to uproot only one vice each year, we would soon become perfect. The contrary, however, is often the case—we feel that we were better and purer in the first fervor of our conversion than we are after many years in the practice of our faith. Our fervor and progress ought to increase day by day. But it is now considered noteworthy if we can retain even a part of our first fervor.

If we were a little severe with ourselves at the start, we would afterward be able to do all things with ease and joy. It is hard to break old habits, but harder still to go against our will.

If you do not overcome small, trifling things, how will you overcome the more difficult? Resist temptations in the beginning, and unlearn the evil habit lest perhaps, little by little, it lead to a more evil one.

If you only consider what peace a good life will bring you and what joy it will give others, I think you will be more concerned about your spiritual progress.

It is good for us to have trials and troubles at times, for they often remind us that we are on probation and ought not to hope in any worldly thing. It is good for us sometimes to suffer contradiction, to be misjudged by others even though we do well and mean well. These things help us to be humble and shield us from vanity. When to all outward appearances others give us no credit, when they do not think well of us, then we are more inclined to seek God, who sees our hearts. Therefore, we ought to root ourselves so firmly in God that we will not need human consolations.

When people of goodwill are afflicted, tempted, and tormented by evil thoughts, they realize clearly that their greatest need is God, without whom they can do no good. Saddened by their miseries and sufferings, they lament and pray. They weary of living longer and wish for death that they might be dissolved and be with Christ. Then they understand fully that perfect security and complete peace cannot be found on earth.

 # TEMPTATIONS

As long as we live in this world we cannot escape suffering and temptation. So it is written in Job: "Do not human beings have a hard service on earth?" All, therefore, must guard against temptation and must watch in prayer so that *the devil,* who *prowls around looking for someone to devour,* will find no occasion to deceive them. None are so perfect or so holy that they are never tempted. We cannot be altogether free from temptation.

Yet temptations, though troublesome and severe, are often useful to us, for in them we are humbled, purified, and instructed. The saints all passed through many temptations and trials and profited by them, while those who could not resist fell away. There is no state so holy, no place so secret, that temptations and trials will not come. We are never safe from them as long as we live, for they come from within us—in sin we were born. When one temptation or trial passes, another comes; we will always have something to suffer because we have lost the state of original blessedness.

Many people try to escape temptations, only to fall more deeply. We cannot conquer simply by fleeing. But by patience and true humility we become stronger than all our enemies. Those who only shun temptations outwardly and do not uproot them will make little progress. Indeed, temptations will quickly return, more violent than before.

Little by little, in patience and long-suffering you will overcome them, by the help of God rather than by severity and your own rash ways. Often seek advice when tempted; and do not be harsh with others who are tempted, but console them as you yourself would wish to be consoled.

The beginning of all temptation lies in a wavering mind and little trust in God, for as a rudderless ship is driven hither and yon by waves, so a careless and irresolute person is tempted in many ways. Fire tempers iron and temptation steels the just. Often we do not know what we can stand, but temptation shows us what we are.

Above all, we must be especially alert against the beginnings of temptation, for the enemy is more easily conquered if he is refused admittance to the mind and is met beyond the threshold when he knocks.

Someone has said very aptly: "Resist the beginnings; remedies come too late, when by long delay the evil has gained strength." First, a mere thought comes to mind, then strong imagination, followed by pleasure, evil delight, and consent. Thus, because he is not resisted in the beginning, Satan gains full entry. And the longer we delay in resisting, so much the weaker do we become each day, while the strength of the enemy grows against us.

Some suffer great temptations in the beginning of their conversion, others toward the end, while some are troubled almost constantly throughout their lives. Others, again, are only tempted lightly according to the wisdom and justice of Divine Providence who weighs the status and merit of each and prepares all for the salvation of God's elect.

We should not despair, therefore, when we are tempted, but pray to God even more fervently that God may see fit to help us. According to the word of Paul, with testing God *will also provide the way out so that you may be able to endure it.* Let us humble our souls under the hand of God in every trial and temptation, for God will save and exalt the humble in spirit.

Our progress is measured in temptations and trials. Opportunity for merit and virtue is made more manifest in them.

When we are not troubled it is not hard for us to be fervent and devout, but if we bear up patiently in time of adversity, there is hope for great progress.

Some, guarded against great temptations, are frequently overcome by small ones so that, humbled by their weakness in small trials, they may not presume on their own strength in great ones.

 **SUFFERING**

Wherever you are, wherever you go, you are miserable unless you turn to God. So why be dismayed when things do not happen as you wish and desire? Is there anyone who has everything one wishes? No—neither I, nor you, nor anyone on earth. There is no one in the world, not even pope or king, who does not suffer trial and anguish.

Who is the better off then? Surely, it is one who will suffer something for God. Many unstable and weak-minded people say: "See how well that man lives, how rich, how great he is, how powerful and mighty." But you must lift up your eyes to the riches of heaven and realize that the material goods of which they speak are nothing. These things are uncertain and very burdensome because they are never possessed without anxiety and fear. Happiness does not consist in the possession of abundant goods. A very little is enough.

Living on earth is truly a misery. The more people desire spiritual life, the more bitter the present becomes to them, because they understand better and see more clearly the defects and corruption of human nature. To eat and drink, to watch and sleep, to rest, to labor, and to be bound by other human necessities are certainly great miseries and afflictions to the devout, who would gladly be released from them and be free from all sin. Truly, the inner self is greatly burdened in this world by the necessities of the body, and for this reason the Prophet prayed that he might be as free from them as possible, when he said, "Bring me out of my distress."

But woe to those who know not their own misery, and greater woe to those who love this miserable and corruptible life. Some, indeed, can scarcely procure its necessities either by work or by begging; yet they love it so much that, if they could live here always, they would care nothing for the kingdom of God.

How foolish and faithless of heart are those who are so caught up in earthly things that they can enjoy only what is physical! Miserable, indeed, for in the end they will see to their sorrow how cheap and worthless was the thing they loved.

The saints of God and all devout friends of Christ did not look to what pleases the body or to the things that are popular from time to time. Their whole hope and aim centered on the everlasting good. Their whole desire pointed upward to the lasting and invisible realm, so that the love of what is visible would not drag them down to lower things.

Do not lose heart, then, in pursuing your spiritual life. There is yet time, and your hour is not past. Why delay your purpose? Arise! Begin at once and say: "Now is the time to act, now is the time to fight, now is the proper time to amend."

When you are troubled and afflicted, that is the time to gain merit. You must pass through water and fire before coming to rest. Unless you discipline yourself you will not overcome vice.

So long as we live in this fragile body, we can neither be free from sin nor live without weariness and sorrow. We would be glad to rest from all misery, but in losing innocence through sin we also lost true blessedness. Therefore, we must have patience and await the mercy of God until this evil passes, until mortality is swallowed up in life.

How great is the frailty of human nature, always tending to evil! Today you confess your sins and tomorrow you again commit the sins that you confessed. One moment you resolve to be careful, and yet after an hour you act as though you had made no resolution.

We have cause, therefore, because of our frailty and feebleness, to humble ourselves and never think anything great of ourselves. Through neglect we may quickly lose what we have acquired by God's grace and only through long, hard labor. What will eventually become of us who grow lukewarm so quickly? Woe to us if we presume to rest in peace and security when actually there is no true holiness in our lives.

REMEMBER THAT YOU ARE DUST

From Book I, Chapter 23

Very soon your life here will end. Consider, then, what may be in store for you elsewhere. Today we live; tomorrow we die and are quickly forgotten. Oh, the dullness and hardness of a heart that looks only to the present instead of preparing for what is to come!

Therefore, in every deed and every thought, act as though you were to die this very day. If you had a good conscience, you would not fear death very much. It is better to avoid sin than to fear death. If you are not prepared today, how will you be prepared tomorrow? Tomorrow is an uncertain day; how do you know you will have a tomorrow?

What good is it to live a long life when we amend that life so little? Indeed, a long life does not always benefit us but, on the contrary, frequently adds to our guilt. If only in this world we had lived well throughout one single day! Many count up the years they have spent in religion but find their lives made little holier. If it is so terrifying to die, it is nevertheless possible that to live longer is more dangerous. Blessed are those who always keep the moment of death before their eyes and prepare for it every day.

If you have ever seen someone die, remember that you, too, must go the same way. In the morning consider that you may not live till evening. When evening comes, do not dare to promise yourself the dawn. Always be ready, therefore, and live in such a way that death will never take you unprepared. Many die suddenly and unexpectedly, for in the unexpected hour the Son of God will come. When that last moment arrives you will begin to have a quite different opinion of the life that is now entirely past and you will regret very much that you were so careless and neglectful.

How happy and prudent are those who try now in life to be what they want to be when found in death. Perfect contempt of the world, a lively desire to advance in virtue, a love for discipline, the works of penance, readiness to obey, self-denial, and the endurance of every hardship for the love of Christ, these will give people great expectations of a happy death.

You can do many good works when in good health. What can you do when you are ill? Few are made better by sickness. Likewise those who undertake many pilgrimages seldom become holy.

Do not put your trust in friends and relatives, and do not put off the care of your soul till later. People will forget you more quickly than you think. It is better to provide now, in time, and send some good account ahead of you than to rely on the help of others. If you do not care for your own welfare now, who will care when you are gone?

The present is very precious. These are the

days of salvation. *Now is the acceptable time.* How sad that you do not spend the time in which you might purchase everlasting life in a better way. The time will come when you will want just one day, just one hour in which to make amends, and do you know whether you will obtain it?

See, then, dearly beloved, the great danger from which you can free yourself and the great fear from which you can be saved, if only you will always be wary and mindful of death. Try to live now in such a manner that at the moment of death you may be glad rather than fearful. Learn to die to the world now, that then you may begin to live with Christ. Learn to spurn all things now, that then you may freely go to him. Punish your body in penance now, that then you may have the confidence born of certainty.

Oh, you fool, why do you plan to live long when you are not sure of living even a day? How many have been deceived and suddenly snatched away! How often have you heard of persons being killed by drowning, by fatal falls from high places, of persons dying at meals, at play, in fires, by the sword, in pestilence, or at the hands of robbers! Death is the end of everyone and human life quickly passes away like a shadow.

Who will remember you when you are dead? Who will pray for you? Do now, beloved, what you can, because you do not know when you will die, nor what your fate will be after death. Gather for yourself the riches of immortality while you have time. Think of nothing but your salvation. Care only for the things of God. Make friends for yourself now by honoring the saints of God, by imitating their actions, so that when you depart this life they may receive you into everlasting dwellings.

Keep yourself as a stranger here on earth, a pilgrim whom its affairs do not concern at all. Keep your heart free and raise it up to God, for you have not here a lasting home. Direct your daily prayers, your sighs and tears, to God, so that your soul may merit after death to pass in happiness to the Lord.

 # PAYING ATTENTION TO THE INNER LIFE

From Book II, Chapters 4 and 5

The second book of The Imitation *is a short treatise on the inner life.*

We are raised up from the earth by two wings—simplicity and purity. There must be simplicity in our intention and purity in our desires. Simplicity leads to God, purity embraces and enjoys God.

If your heart is free from ill-ordered affection, no good deed will be difficult for you. If you aim at and seek after nothing but the pleasure of God and the welfare of your neighbor, you will enjoy freedom within.

If your heart were right, then every created thing would be a mirror of life for you and a book of holy teaching. There is no creature so small and worthless that it does not show forth the goodness of God. If inwardly you were good and pure, you would see all things clearly and understand them rightly. A pure heart penetrates to heaven and hell, and as we are within, so we judge what is without. If there is joy in the world, the pure of heart certainly possess it. If there is anguish and affliction anywhere, an evil conscience knows it too well.

As iron cast into fire loses its rust and becomes glowing white, so those who turn completely to God are stripped of their sluggishness and changed into new people. When people begin to grow lazy, they fear a little labor and welcome external comfort. But when they begin to conquer themselves perfectly and to walk bravely in the ways of God, then they think those things less difficult that they thought to be so hard before.

We must not rely too much upon ourselves, for grace and understanding are often lacking in us. We have but little inborn light, and this we quickly lose through negligence. Often we are not aware that we are so blind in heart. Meanwhile we do wrong, and then do worse in excusing it. At times we are moved by passion, and we think it zeal. We take others to task for small mistakes, and overlook greater ones in ourselves. We are quick enough to feel and brood over the things we suffer from others, but we think nothing of how much others suffer from us. If we would weigh our own deeds fully and rightly, we would find little cause to pass severe judgment on others.

Inward-directed people put the care of themselves before all other concerns. Those who attend to themselves carefully do not find it hard to hold their tongues about others. You will never be devout of heart unless you are thus silent about the affairs of others and pay particular attention to yourself. If you attend wholly to God and yourself, you will be little disturbed by what you see about you.

Where are your thoughts when they are not upon yourself? And after attending to various things, what have you gained if you have neglected yourself? If you wish to have true peace of mind and unity of purpose, you must cast all else aside and keep only yourself before your eyes.

You will make great progress if you keep yourself free from all temporal cares, for to value anything that is temporal is a great mistake. Consider nothing great, nothing high, nothing pleasing, nothing acceptable, except God or what comes from God. Consider the consolations of creatures as vanity. The soul that loves God scorns all lesser things. God alone, the eternal and infinite, satisfies all, bringing comfort to the soul and true joy to the body.

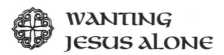

WANTING JESUS ALONE

From Book II, Chapters 7 and 8

Blessed are those who appreciate what it is to love Jesus and who despise themselves for the sake of Jesus. Give up all other love for his, since he wishes to be loved alone above all things.

Affection for creatures is deceitful and inconstant, but the love of Jesus is true and enduring. Those who cling to a creature will fall with its frailty, but those who give themselves to Jesus will always be strengthened.

Love him, then. Keep him as a friend. He will not leave you as others do, or let you suffer lasting death. Sometime, whether or not you want it, you will have to part with everything. Cling, therefore, to Jesus in life and death. Trust yourself to the glory of the only One who can help you when all others fail.

Your Beloved is such that he will not accept what belongs to another. He wants your heart for himself alone, to be enthroned there as King in his own right. If you only knew how to free yourself entirely from all creatures, Jesus would gladly dwell within you.

You will find that, apart from him, nearly all the trust you place in people is a total loss. Therefore, neither confide in nor depend upon a wind-shaken reed, for *all people are grass* and their glory, like the flower of grass, will fade away.

You will quickly be deceived if you look only to the outward appearance of others, and you will often be disappointed if you seek comfort and gain in them. If, however, you seek Jesus in all things, you will surely find him. Likewise, if you seek yourself, you will find yourself—to your own ruin. For those who do not seek Jesus do themselves much greater harm than the whole world and all their enemies could ever do.

When Jesus is near, all is well and nothing seems difficult. When he is absent, all is hard. When Jesus does not speak within, all other comfort is empty, but if he says only a word, it brings great consolation.

Did not Mary rise at once from her weeping when Martha said to her, *The Teacher is here and is calling for you*? Happy is the hour when Jesus calls one from tears to joy of spirit.

How dry and hard you are without Jesus! How foolish and vain if you desire anything but him! Is it not a greater loss than losing the whole world? For what, without Jesus, can the world give you? Life without him is a relentless hell, but living with him is a sweet paradise. If Jesus is with you, no enemy can harm you.

Whoever finds Jesus finds a rare treasure, indeed, a good above every good. But whoever loses Jesus loses more than the whole world. Those who live without Jesus are the poorest of the poor, whereas no one is so rich as one who lives in his grace.

It is a great art to know how to converse with Jesus, and great wisdom to know how to keep him. Be humble and peaceful, and Jesus will be with you. Be devout and calm, and he will remain with you. You may quickly drive him away and lose his grace if you turn back to the outside world. And if you drive him away and lose him, to whom will you go and whom will you then seek as a friend? You cannot live well without a friend, and if Jesus is not your best friend, you will be very sad and desolate. Thus, you are acting foolishly if you trust or rejoice in any other. Choose the opposition of the whole world rather than offend Jesus. Of all those who are dear to you, let him be your special love. Let all things be loved for the sake of Jesus, but Jesus for his own sake.

Jesus Christ must be loved alone with a special love for he alone of all friends, is good and faithful. For him and in him you must love friends and foes alike, and pray to him that all may know and love him.

Never desire special praise or love, for that belongs to God alone who has no equal. Never wish that anyone's affection be centered in you, nor let yourself be taken up with the love of anyone, but let Jesus be in you and in every good person. Be pure and free within, not entangled with any creature.

You must bring to God a clean and open heart if you wish to see how sweet the Lord is. Truly you will never attain this happiness unless God's grace prepares you and draws you on so that you may forsake all things to be united with him alone.

When the grace of God comes to people, they can do all things, but when it leaves them, they become poor and weak, as if abandoned to affliction. Yet in this condition they should not become dejected or despair. On the contrary, they should calmly await the will of God and bear whatever befalls them in praise of Jesus Christ, for after winter comes summer, after night, the day, and after the storm, a great calm.

BEARING THE CROSS OF CHRIST

From Book II, Chapters 11 and 12

Jesus has always many who love his heavenly kingdom, but few who bear his cross. He has many who desire consolation, but few who care for trial. He finds many to share his table, but few to take part in his fasting. All desire to be happy with him; few wish to suffer anything for him. Many follow him to the breaking of bread, but few to the drinking of the chalice of his passion. Many revere his miracles; few approach the shame of the Cross. Many love him as long as they encounter no hardship; many praise and bless him as long as they receive some comfort from him. But if Jesus hides himself and leaves them for a while, they fall either into complaints or into deep dejection. Those, on the contrary, who love him for his own sake and not for any comfort of their own, bless him in all trial and anguish of heart as well as in the bliss of consolation. Even if he never gives them consolation, yet they would continue to praise him and wish always to give him thanks. What power there is in pure love for Jesus—love that is free from all self-interest and self-love!

Do not those who always seek consolation deserve to be called mercenaries? Do not those who always think of their own profit and gain prove that they love themselves rather than Christ? Where can anyone be found who desires to serve God for nothing? Rarely indeed are people so spiritual as to strip themselves of all things. And who will find anyone so truly poor in spirit as to be free from every creature? Such a person's value is like that of things brought from the most distant lands.

If we give all our wealth, it is nothing. If we do great penance, it is little. If we gain all knowledge, we are still far afield. If we have great virtue and much ardent devotion, we still lack a great deal — especially the one thing we need most. What is this one thing? That leaving all, we forsake ourselves, completely renounce ourselves, and give up all private affections. Then when we have done all that we know ought to be done, let us consider it as nothing. Let us make little of what may be considered great. Let us in all honesty call ourselves worthless slaves. For truth itself has said: *When you have done all that you were ordered to do, say: "we are worthless slaves."*

Then we will be truly poor and stripped in spirit, and with the prophet may say: *I am lonely and afflicted.* None, however, are more wealthy than such people. None are more powerful, none freer than those who know how to leave all things and think of themselves as the least of all.

To many the saying, *Deny* yourself *and take up the cross and follow me*, seems hard, but it will be much harder to hear that final word: *You that are accursed, depart from me into the eternal fire.* Those who hear the word of the Cross and follow it willingly now need not fear that they will hear of eternal damnation on the day of judgment. This sign of the Cross will be in the heavens when the Lord comes to judge. Then all the servants of the Cross, who during life made themselves one with the Crucified, will draw near with great trust to Christ, the judge.

Why, then, do you fear to take up the cross when through it you can win a kingdom? In the Cross is salvation. In the Cross is life. In the Cross is protection from enemies. In the Cross is infusion of heavenly sweetness. In the Cross is strength of mind. In the Cross is joy of spirit. In the Cross is highest virtue. In the Cross is perfect holiness. There is no salvation of soul nor hope of everlasting life but in the Cross.

If you carry the cross willingly, it will carry and lead you to the desired goal where indeed there shall be no more suffering, though here there will be. If you carry it unwillingly, you create a burden for yourself and increase the load, though still you have to bear it. If you cast away one cross, you will find another and perhaps a heavier one. Do you expect to escape what no mortal can ever avoid? Which of the saints was without a cross or trial on this earth?

The whole life of Christ was a cross and a martyrdom. Do you, then, seek rest and enjoyment for yourself? You deceive yourself and are mistaken if you seek anything but to suffer. This mortal life is full of miseries and marked with crosses on all sides.

Indeed, the more spiritual progress people make, the heavier will they find the cross. As their love increases, the pain of their exile also increases.

Yet such people, though afflicted in many ways, are not without hope of consolation. They know that great reward is coming to them for bearing the cross. And when they carry it willingly, every pang of tribulation is changed into hope of comfort from God. Nothing is more acceptable to God, nothing more helpful for you on this earth than to suffer willingly for Christ. If you had to make a choice, you ought to wish rather to suffer for Christ than to enjoy many consolations. In this way you would be more like Christ and more like all the saints.

When, therefore, we have read and searched all that has been written, let this be the final conclusion: *It is through many persecutions that we must enter the kingdom of God.*

DISCRETION AND HUMILITY

The third book of The Imitation *is a dialogue between Christ and the Christian disciple. In this passage, Christ speaks.*

It is better and safer for you to conceal the grace of devotion. Do not be elated by it or speak or think much of it. Instead, humble yourself and fear that it is being given to one unworthy of it. Do not cling too closely to this affection, for it may quickly be changed to its opposite. When you are in grace, think how miserable and needy you are without it. Your progress in spiritual life does not consist in having the grace of consolation, but in enduring its withdrawal with humility, resignation, and patience. Then you will not become listless in prayer or neglect your other duties in the least. On the contrary, do what you can do as well as you know how and do not neglect yourself completely because of your dryness or anxiety of mind.

There are many, indeed, who immediately become impatient and lazy when things do not go well with them. The human way, however, does not always lie in our own power. It is God's prerogative to give grace and to console when God wishes, as much as God wishes, and whom God wishes, as it pleases God and no more.

Some careless persons, misusing the grace of devotion, have destroyed themselves because they wished to do more than they were able. They failed to take account of their own weakness, and followed the desire of their heart rather than the judgment of their reason. Then, because they presumed to greater things than pleased God, they quickly lost God's grace. They who had built their homes in heaven became helpless, vile outcasts, humbled and impoverished. And so they learned not to fly with their own wings but to trust in mine.

Those who are still new and inexperienced in the way of the Lord may easily be deceived and overthrown unless they guide themselves by the advice of discreet persons. But if they wish to follow their own notions rather than to trust in others who are more experienced, they will be in danger of a sorry end, at least if they are unwilling to be drawn from their vanity. Seldom do those who are wise in their own opinions bear the guidance of others humbly. Yet a little knowledge humbly and meekly pursued is better than great treasures of learning sought in vain complacency. It is better for you to have little than to have much that may become the source of pride.

Those who give themselves up entirely to enjoyment act very unwisely, for they forget their former helplessness and the chastened fear of the Lord that dreads to lose a proffered grace. Those who become too despondent in times of adversity and difficulty and think less confidently of me than they should are not very brave or wise. Those who wish to be too secure in time of peace will often become too dejected and fearful in time of trial.

If you were wise enough to remain always humble and small in your own eyes, and to restrain and rule your spirit well, you would not fall so quickly into danger and offense.

When a spirit of fervor is enkindled within you, you may well meditate on how you will feel when the fervor leaves. Then, when this happens, remember that the light that I have withdrawn for a time as a warning to you and for my own glory may again return. Such trials are often more beneficial than if you had things always as you wish. For your merits are not measured by many visions or consolations, or by knowledge of the Scriptures, or by your being in a higher position than others, but by the truth of your humility, by your capacity for divine love, by your constancy in seeking purely and entirely the honor of God, by your disregard and positive contempt of self, and more, by preferring to be despised and humiliated rather than honored by others.

the heart's desires

From Book III, Chapters 11 and 12

CHRIST: My child, it is necessary for you to learn many things that you have not yet learned well.

DISCIPLE: What are they, Lord?

CHRIST: That you conform your desires entirely according to my good pleasure, and be not a lover of self but an earnest doer of my will. Desires very often inflame you and drive you madly on, but consider whether you act for my honor or for your own advantage. If I am the cause, you will be well content with whatever I ordain. If, on the other hand, any self-seeking lurks in you, it troubles you and weighs you down. Take care, then, that you do not rely too much on preconceived desire that has no reference to me, so that you need not repent later on and be displeased with what at first pleased you and that you desired as being for the best. Not every desire that seems good should be followed immediately, nor, on the other hand, should every contrary affection be at once rejected.

It is sometimes well to use a little restraint even in good desires and inclinations. Otherwise you might bring upon yourself mental distraction through too much eagerness or create scandal for others through your lack of discipline or be suddenly upset and fall because of resistance from others. Sometimes, however, you must be strong and resist your sensual appetite bravely. You must pay no attention to what the flesh does or does not desire, taking pains to subject it, even by force, to the spirit. Chastise it and force it to remain in subjection until it is prepared for anything and is taught to be satisfied with little, to take pleasure in simple things, and not to grumble about inconveniences.

DISCIPLE: Patience, O Lord God, is very necessary for me, I see, because there are many hardships in this life. No matter what plans I make for my own peace, my life cannot be free from struggle and sorrow.

CHRIST: My child, you are right, yet my wish is not that you seek a peace that is free from temptations or meets with no opposition, but rather that you consider yourself as having found peace when you have been tormented with many tribulations and tried with many hardships.

Do you think that worldly people have no suffering, or perhaps but little? Ask even those who enjoy the most delights and you will learn otherwise. "But," you will say, "they enjoy many pleasures and follow their own wishes. Therefore they do not feel their troubles very much." Granted that they do have whatever they wish, how long do you think it will last? Behold, those who prosper in the world will perish like smoke, and there will be no memory of their past joys. Even in this life they do not find rest in these pleasures without bitterness, weariness, and fear. For they often receive the penalty of sorrow from what they believe is the source of their happiness. And it is just. Since they seek and follow after pleasures without reason, they should not enjoy them without shame and bitterness.

How brief, how false, how unreasonable and shameful all these pleasures are! Yet in their drunken blindness people do not understand this, but like brute beasts incur death of soul for the miserly enjoyment of a corruptible life.

Therefore, my child, *do not follow your base desires*, but turn away from your own will. *Take delight in the Lord, and he will give you the desires of your heart.* If you wish to be truly delighted and more abundantly comforted by me, behold, your blessing will be found in contempt of all worldly things and in the cutting off of all base pleasures, and great consolation will be given you. Further, the more you withdraw yourself from any comfort from creatures, the sweeter and stronger comfort you will find in me.

At first you will not gain these blessings without sadness and toil and conflict. Habit already formed will resist you, but it will be overcome by a better habit. The flesh will murmur against you, but it will be bridled by fervor of spirit. The old serpent will sting and trouble you, but prayer will put it to flight. By steadfast, useful toil the way will be closed to it.

them. Keep me from many necessities of the body, lest I be ensnared by pleasure. Keep me from all darkness of mind, lest I be broken by troubles and overcome. I do not ask deliverance from those things that worldly vanity desires so eagerly, but from those miseries that, by the common curse of humankind, oppress the souls of your servants in punishment and keep them from entering into the liberty of spirit as often as they would.

My God, sweetness beyond words, make bitter all the carnal comfort that draws me from love of the eternal and lures me to its evil self by the sight of some delightful good in the present. Let it not overcome me, my God. Let not flesh and blood conquer me. Let not the world and its brief glory deceive me, nor the devil trip me by his craftiness. Give me courage to resist, patience to endure, and constancy to persevere. Give me the soothing unction of your Spirit rather than all the consolations of the world, and in place of carnal love, infuse into me the love of your name.

See how burdensome eating, drinking, clothing, and other necessities that sustain the body are to the fervent soul. Grant me the grace to use such comforts temperately and not to become entangled in too great a desire for them. It is not lawful to cast them aside completely, for nature must be sustained. But your holy law forbids us to demand unnecessary things and things that are simply for pleasure. Otherwise the flesh would rebel against the spirit. In these matters, I beg, let your hand guide and direct me, so that I may not overstep the law in any way.

# SPIRITUAL FREEDOM

From Book III, Chapters 31 and 32

DISCIPLE: O Lord, I am in sore need still of greater grace if I am to arrive at the point where no person and no created thing can be an obstacle to me. For as long as anything holds me back, I cannot freely fly to you. The one who said *Oh that I had wings like a dove! I would fly away and be at rest*, desired to fly freely to you. Who is more at rest than one who aims at nothing but God? And who more free than one who desires nothing on earth?

It is well, then, to pass over all creation, perfectly to abandon self, and to see in ecstasy of mind that you, the creator of all, have no likeness among all your creatures, and that unless we are freed from all creatures, we cannot attend freely to the divine. The reason why so few contemplative persons are found is that so few know how to separate themselves entirely from what is transitory and created.

For this, indeed, great grace is needed, grace that will raise the soul and lift it up above itself. Unless we are elevated in spirit, free from all creatures, and completely united to God, all our knowledge and possessions are of little importance. Those who consider anything great except the one, immense, eternal good will remain little and lie groveling on the earth. Whatever is not God is nothing and must be accounted as nothing.

There is great difference between the wisdom of an enlightened and devout person and the learning of a well-read and brilliant scholar, for the knowledge that flows down from divine sources is much nobler than that laboriously acquired by human industry.

Many there are who desire contemplation, but who do not care to do the things that contemplation requires. It is also a great obstacle to be satisfied with externals and sensible things, and to have so little of perfect mortification. I do not know what it is, or by what spirit we are led, or to what we pretend—we who wish to be called spiritual—that we spend so much labor and even more anxiety on things that are transitory and low, while we seldom or never turn with full consciousness to our interior concerns.

Alas, after very little recollection we falter, not weighing our deeds by strict examination. We pay no attention to where our affections lie, nor do we deplore the fact that our actions are impure.

Remember that because *all flesh had corrupted its ways*, the great deluge followed. Since, then, our interior affection is corrupt, it must be that the action that follows from it, the outward indicator of our lack of inward strength, is also corrupt. Out of a pure heart come the fruits of a good life.

People usually ask how much others have done, but they think little of the virtue with which they act. They ask: Are they strong? rich? handsome? good writers? good singers? or good workers? They say little, however, about how poor they are in spirit, how patient and meek, how devout and spiritual. Nature looks to outward appearance; grace turns to inward being. The one often errs, the other trusts in God and is not deceived.

CHRIST: My child, you can never be perfectly free unless you completely renounce self, for all who seek their own interest and who love themselves are bound in fetters. They are unsettled by covetousness and curiosity, always searching for ease and not for the things of Christ, often devising and framing what will not last, for anything that is not of God will fail completely.

Hold to this short and perfect advice, therefore: give up your desires and you will find rest. Think about it in your heart, and when you have put it into practice you will understand all things.

DISCIPLE: But this, Lord, is not the work of one day, nor is it mere child's play. Indeed, in this brief sentence is included all the perfection of holy persons.

CHRIST: My child, you should not turn away or be downcast when you hear the way of the perfect. Rather you ought to be spurred on the more toward their sublime heights or at least be moved to seek perfection.

I would this were the case with you—that you had progressed to the point where you no longer loved self but simply awaited my bidding and God's, whom I have placed as father over you. Then you would please me very much, and your whole life would pass in peace and joy. But you have yet many things that you must give up, and unless you resign them entirely to me you will not obtain what you ask.

I counsel you to buy from me gold refined by fire so that you may be rich—rich in heavenly wisdom that treads underfoot all that is low. Put aside earthly wisdom, all human self-complacency.

I have said to exchange what is precious and valued among people for what is considered contemptible. For true heavenly wisdom—not to think highly of self and not to seek glory on earth—does indeed seem low and small and is nearly forgotten. Many praise it with their mouths but shy far away from it in their lives. Yet this heavenly wisdom is a *pearl of great value* and hidden from many.

ḃAPPINESS AND JOY IN GOD

CHRIST: My child, do not trust in your present feeling, for it will soon give way to another. As long as you live you will be changeable in spite of yourself. You will become happy at one time and sad at another, now peaceful but again disturbed, at one moment devout and the next not, sometimes diligent while at other times lazy, now serious and again flippant.

But those who are wise and whose spirits are well instructed stand superior to these changes. They pay no attention to what they feel in themselves or from what quarter the wind of fickleness blows. The whole intention of their minds is directed to their proper and desired end. So they can stand undivided, unchanged, and unshaken, with singleness of intention directed unwaveringly toward me, even in the midst of so many changing events. And the purer this singleness of intention is, with so much more constancy do they pass through many storms.

DISCIPLE: Behold, my God and my all! What more do I wish for? What greater happiness can I desire? O sweet and delicious word! But sweet only to those who love it, and not to the world or the things that are in the world.

My God and my all! These words are enough for those who understand, and for those who love, it is a joy to repeat them often. For when you are present, all things are delightful. When you are absent, all things become loathsome. It is you who give a heart tranquillity, great peace, and festive joy. It is you who make us think well of all things, and praise you in all things. Without you nothing can give pleasure for very long, for if it is to be pleasing and tasteful, your grace and the seasoning of your wisdom must be in it. What is there that can displease one whose happiness is in you? And on the contrary, what can satisfy one whose delight is not in you?

The wise people of the world, those who lust for the flesh, are lacking in your wisdom, because in the world is found the utmost vanity, and in the flesh is death. But those who follow you by disdaining worldly things and mortifying the flesh are known to be truly wise, for they are transported from vanity to truth, from flesh to spirit. By such as these God is relished, and whatever good is found in creatures they turn to praise of the Creator. But the difference is great—yes, very great, indeed—between delight in the Creator and in the creature, in eternity and in time, in Light uncreated and in the light that is reflected.

O Light eternal, surpassing all created brightness, flash forth the lightning from above and enlighten the inmost recesses of my heart. Cleanse, cheer, enlighten, and enliven my spirit with all its powers, that it may cling to you in ecstasies of joy. Oh, when will that happy and wished-for hour come, when you will fill me with your presence and become all in all to me? So long as this is not given me, my joy will not be complete.

The old Adam, alas, still lives within me. He has not yet been entirely crucified. He is not yet entirely dead. He still lusts strongly against the spirit, and will not leave the kingdom of my soul in peace. But you, who can command the power of the sea and calm the tumult of its waves, arise and help me. Scatter the nations that delight in war. Crush them in your sight. Please, show forth your wonderful works and let your right hand be glorified, because there is no other hope or refuge for me except in you, O Lord, my God.

CHRIST'S FAITHFULNESS

From Book III, Chapter 46

The "holy soul" quoted below is Saint Agatha of Catania, Sicily. The words are taken from the story of her life as read on her feast day.

DISCIPLE: *O grant us help against the foe, for human help is worthless.* How often have I failed to find faithfulness in places where I thought I possessed it! And how many times I have found it where I least expected it! Vain, therefore, is hope in people, but the salvation of the just is in you, O God. Blessed be your name, O Lord my God, in everything that befalls us.

We are weak and unstable, quickly deceived and changed. Who can guard themselves with such caution and care as not sometimes to fall into deception or perplexity? Those who confide in you, O Lord, and seek you with a simple heart do not fall so easily. And if some trouble should come upon them, no matter how entangled in it they may be, they will more quickly be delivered and comforted by you. For you will not forsake any who trust in you to the very end.

Rare is the person who remains faithful through all a friend's distress. But you, Lord, and you alone, are entirely faithful in all things; other than you, there is none so faithful.

Oh, how wise is that holy soul who said: "My mind is firmly settled and founded in Christ." If that were true of me, human fear would not so easily cause me anxiety, nor would the darts of words disturb. But who can foresee all things and provide against all evils? And if things foreseen have often hurt, how can unexpected things not wound us seriously? Why, indeed, have I not provided better for my wretched self? Why, too, have I so easily kept faith in others?

In whom shall I put my faith, Lord? In whom but you? You are the truth that does not deceive and cannot be deceived. Every human being, on the other hand, is a liar, weak, unstable, and likely to err, especially in words, so that one ought not to be too quick to believe even what seems, on the face of it, to sound true. How wise was your warning to beware of other people; that *one's foes will be members of one's own household;* that *if anyone says, "Look! Here is the Messiah!" or "There he is!"*—we should *not believe it.*

I have been taught to my own cost, and I hope it has given me greater caution, not greater folly. "Beware," they say, "beware and keep to yourself what I tell you!" Then while I keep silent, believing that the matter is secret, those who ask me to be silent cannot remain silent themselves, but immediately betray both me and themselves and go their way. From tales of this kind and from such uncaring people protect me, O Lord, lest I fall into their hands and into their ways. Put in my mouth words that are true and steadfast and keep the crafty tongue far from me. I should certainly shun what I am not willing to endure.

Oh, how good and how peaceful it is to be silent about others, not to believe without discrimination all that is said, not easily to report it further, to reveal oneself to few, always to seek you as the discerner of hearts, and not to be blown away by every wind of words, but to wish that all things, within and beyond us, be done according to the pleasure of your will.

How helpful it is for the keeping of heavenly grace to fly from the gaze of others, not to go out seeking things that seem to cause admiration, but to follow with utmost diligence those who give fervor and amendment of life! How many have been harmed by having their virtue known and praised too hastily! And how truly profitable it has been when grace remained hidden during this frail life, which is all temptation and warfare!

CHRIST'S JUDGMENT AND MERCY

CHRIST. My child, stand firm and trust in me. For what are words but words? They fly through the air but hurt not a stone. If you are guilty, consider how you would gladly amend. If you are not conscious of any fault, think that you wish to bear this for the sake of God. It is little enough for you occasionally to endure words, since you are not yet strong enough to bear hard blows.

Why do such small matters pierce you to the heart, unless because you are still worldly and pay more attention to others than you ought? You do not wish to be reproved for your faults and you seek shelter in excuses because you are afraid of being despised. But look into yourself more thoroughly and you will learn that the world is still alive in you, in a vain desire to please others. For when you shrink from being put down or embarrassed for your failings, it is plain indeed that you are not truly humble or truly dead to the world, and that the world is not crucified in you.

Listen to my word, and you will not value ten thousand human words. If every malicious thing that could possibly be invented were uttered against you, what harm could it do if you ignored it all and gave it no more thought than you would a blade of grass?

Could it so much as pluck one hair from your head?

Those who do not keep their hearts within them, and who do not have God before their eyes, are easily moved by a word of depreciation. Those who trust in me, on the other hand, and who have no desire to stand by their own judgment, will be free from the fear of others. For I am the judge and discerner of all secrets. I know how all things happen. I know who causes injury and who suffers it. From me that word proceeded, and with my permission it happened, that out of many hearts thoughts may be revealed. I will judge the guilty and the innocent. But I have wished first to try them both by secret judgment.

Human testimony is often deceiving, but my judgment is true. It will stand and not be over-thrown. It is hidden from many and made known to but a few. Yet it is never mistaken and cannot be mistaken even though it does not seem right in the eyes of the unwise.

To me, therefore, you ought to come in every decision, not depending on your own judgment. For the just will not be disturbed, no matter what God may allow to happen to them. Even if an unjust charge is made against them, they will not be troubled much. Neither will they rejoice vainly if they are justly acquitted through others. They know that I search people's hearts and inmost thoughts and do not judge according to the face of things or human appearances. For what human judgment considers praiseworthy is often worthy of blame in my sight.

DISCIPLE: O Lord God, just Judge, strong and patient, you know human weakness and depravity. Be my strength and all my confidence, for my own conscience is not sufficient for me. You know what I do not know, and therefore, I ought to humble myself whenever I am accused and bear it meekly. Forgive me, then, in your mercy for my every failure in this regard, and give me once more the grace of greater endurance. Better to me is your abundant mercy in obtaining pardon than the justice that I imagine in defending the secrets of my conscience. Even though I am not myself conscious of any fault, I still cannot justify myself, because without your mercy *no one living is righteous before you.*

GROWING IN PURITY

CHRIST: My child, when you feel the desire for everlasting happiness poured out upon you from above, and when you long to leave your bodily tent in order to contemplate my glory without threat of change, open wide your heart and receive this holy inspiration eagerly. Give deepest thanks to the heavenly Goodness who deals with you so understandingly, visits you so mercifully, stirs you so fervently, and sustains you so powerfully so that you do not sink down to earthly things under your own weight. For you do not obtain this by your own thought or effort, but simply by the condescension of heavenly grace and divine regard. This is so that you may advance in virtue and in greater humility, that you may prepare yourself for future trials, that you may strive to cling to me with all the affection of your heart and serve me with a fervent will.

My child, often, when the fire is burning the flame does not ascend without smoke. Likewise, the desires of some burn toward heavenly things, and yet they are not free from temptations of worldly affection. Therefore, it is not altogether for the pure honor of God that they act when they petition God so earnestly. Such, too, is often your desire that you profess to be so strong. For what is alloyed with self-interest is not pure and perfect.

Ask, therefore, not for what is pleasing and convenient to yourself, but for what is acceptable to me and is for my honor, because if you judge rightly, you ought to prefer and follow my will, not your own desire or whatever things you wish.

I know your longings and I have heard your frequent sighs. Already you wish to be in the liberty of the glory of God's children. Already you desire the delights of the eternal home, the heavenly land that is full of joy. But that hour is not yet come. There remains yet another hour, a time of war, of labor, and of trial. You long to be filled with the highest good, but you cannot attain it now. I am that sovereign Good. Wait for me, until the kingdom of God comes.

You must still be tested on earth in many things. Consolation will sometimes be given you, but the complete fullness of it is not granted. Take courage, therefore, and be strong both to do and to suffer what is contrary to nature.

You must put on the new person. You must be changed into another person. You must often do the things you do not wish to do and give up those you do wish to do. What pleases others will succeed; what pleases you will not. The words of others will be heard; what you say will be accounted as nothing. Others will ask and receive; you will ask and not receive. Others will gain great fame; about you nothing will be said. To others the doing of this or that will be entrusted; you will be judged useless. In all this, your human nature will sometimes be sad and it will be a great thing if you bear this sadness in silence. For in these and many similar ways the faithful servants of the Lord are tested, to see how far they can deny themselves and break themselves in all things.

But consider, my child, the fruit of these labors, how soon they will end and how greatly they will be rewarded, and you will not be saddened by them, but your patience will receive the strongest consolation. For instead of the little will that you now readily give up, you will always have your will in heaven. There, indeed, you will find all that you could desire. There you will have possession of every good without fear of losing it. There will your will be forever one with mine. It will desire nothing outside of me and nothing for itself. There no one will oppose you or complain about you, and nothing will stand in your way. All that you desire will be present there, replenishing your affection and satisfying it to the full. There I will give you glory for the reproach you have suffered here. For your sorrow I will give you a garment of praise, and for the lowest place a seat of power forever. There the fruit of glory will appear, the labor of penance rejoice, and humble subjection be gloriously crowned.

Bow humbly, therefore, under the will of all, and do not pay attention to who said this or commanded that. But let it be your special care when something is commanded, or even hinted at, whether by a superior or an inferior or an equal, that you take it to heart and try honestly to perform it. Let one person seek one thing and another something else. Let one glory in this, another in that, and both be praised a thousand times over. But as for you, rejoice neither in one nor in the other, but only in contempt of yourself and in my pleasure and honor. Let this be your wish: that whether in life or in death God may be glorified in you.

NATURE AND GRACE

From Book III, Chapter 54

Thomas uses nature and grace as a sort of shorthand to contrast the old self dominated by unfallen human nature with the new self in Christ, transformed by grace.

CHRIST: My child, pay careful attention to the movements of nature and of grace, for they move in very contrary and subtle ways. They can scarcely be distinguished by anyone except one who is spiritual and inwardly enlightened. All people, indeed, desire what is good, and strive for what is good in their words and deeds. For this reason the appearance of good deceives many.

Nature is crafty and attracts many, ensnaring and deceiving them while ever seeking itself. But grace walks in simplicity, turns away from all appearance of evil, offers no deceits, and does all purely for God in whom it rests as its final end.

Nature is not willing to die, or to be kept down, or to be overcome. Nor will it subdue itself or be made subject. Grace, on the contrary, strives for self-denial. It resists sensuality, seeks to be in subjection, longs to be conquered, has no wish to use its own liberty, loves to be held under discipline, and does not desire to rule over anyone, but wishes rather to live, to stand, and to be always under God for whose sake it is willing to bow humbly to every human creature.

Nature works for its own interest and looks to the profit it can reap from another. Grace does not consider what is useful and advantageous to itself, but rather what is profitable to many. Nature likes to receive honor and reverence, but grace faithfully attributes all honor and glory to God. Nature fears shame and contempt, but grace is happy to suffer reproach for the name of Jesus. Nature loves ease and physical rest. Grace, however, cannot bear to be idle and embraces work willingly. Nature seeks to possess what is rare and beautiful, hating things that are cheap and coarse. Grace, on the contrary, delights in simple, humble things, not despising those that are rough, nor refusing to be clothed in old garments.

Nature has an eye for worldly wealth and rejoices in earthly gains. It is sad over a loss and irritated by a slight, injurious word. But grace looks to eternal things and does not cling to those that are temporary, being neither disturbed at loss nor angered by hard words, because it has placed its treasure and joy in heaven where nothing is lost.

Nature is covetous, and receives more willingly than it gives. It loves to have its own private possessions. Grace, however, is kind and openhearted. Grace shuns private interest, is contented with little, and judges it more blessed to give than to receive.

Nature is inclined toward creatures, toward its own flesh, toward vanities, and toward running about. But grace draws near to God and to virtue, renounces creatures, hates the desires of the flesh, restrains its wanderings, and blushes at being seen in public.

Nature likes to have some external comfort in which it can take sensual delight, but grace seeks consolation only in God, to find its delight in the highest good, above all visible things.

Nature does everything for its own gain and interest. It can do nothing without pay and hopes for its good deeds to receive their equal or better, or else praise and favor. It wishes greatly to have its deeds and gifts highly regarded. Grace, however, seeks nothing in this world nor asks any payment but God alone. It asks for no more of the necessities of this life than will serve to obtain eternity.

Nature rejoices in many friends and kinsfolk, glories in noble position and birth, fawns on the powerful, flatters the rich, and applauds those who are like itself. But grace loves even its enemies and is not puffed up at having many friends. It does not think highly of either position or birth unless virtue is also there. It favors the poor in preference to the rich. It sympathizes with the innocent rather than with the powerful. It rejoices with the truthful rather than with the deceitful and is always exhorting the good to strive for better gifts, to become like the Son of God by practicing the virtues.

Nature is quick to complain of need and trouble. Grace bravely puts up with scarcity. Nature turns all things back to the self. It fights and argues for the self. Grace brings all things back to God in whom they have their source. It claims no good for itself and is not arrogant or presumptuous or contentious. It does not prefer its own opinion to the opinion of others, but in every matter of sense and thought submits itself to eternal wisdom and divine judgment.

Nature has a taste for knowing secrets and hearing news. It wishes to be seen and to have many sense experiences. It wishes to be known and to do things for which it will be praised and admired. But grace does not care to hear news or curious matters, because all this arises from humanity's old corruption, since there is nothing new, nothing lasting on earth. Grace teaches, therefore, restraint of the senses, avoidance of vain self-satisfaction and show, humble hiding of deeds worthy of praise and admiration, and seeking in everything and in every knowledge the fruit of usefulness, the praise and honor of God. It will not have itself exalted, but desires that God, who bestows all simply out of love, should be blessed in God's gifts.

This grace is a supernatural light, a certain special gift of God, the proper mark of the elect, and the pledge of everlasting salvation. It raises us up from earthly things to love the things of heaven. It makes a spiritual person of a natural one. The more, then, nature is held in check and conquered, the more grace is given. Every day the interior self is reformed by new visitations according to the image of God.

NEED FOR GOD'S GRACE

DISCIPLE: O Lord, my God, who created me in your own image and likeness, grant me this grace that you have shown to be so great and necessary for salvation, that I may overcome my very evil nature that is drawing me to sin and perdition. For I feel in my flesh the law of sin contradicting the law of my mind and leading me captive to serve sensuality in many things. I cannot resist my passions unless your most holy grace, warmly infused into my heart, assists me.

There is need of your grace, and of great grace, in order to overcome a nature prone to evil from youth. For through the first man, Adam, nature is fallen and weakened by sin, and the punishment of that stain has fallen upon all humankind. Thus nature itself, which you created good and right, is considered a symbol of vice and the weakness of corrupted nature, because when left to itself it tends toward evil and to baser things. The little strength remaining in it is like a spark hidden in ashes. That strength is natural reason that, surrounded by thick darkness, still has the power of judging good and evil, of seeing the difference between true and false, though it is not able to fulfill all that it approves and does not enjoy the full light of truth or soundness of affection.

So it is, my God, that *I delight in* your *law in my inmost self,* knowing that your *commandment is holy and just and good,* and that it proves the necessity of shunning all evil and sin. But in the flesh I keep *the law of sin,* obeying sensuality rather than reason. So, also, *I can will what is right, but I cannot do it.* So, too, I often propose many good things, but because the grace to help my weakness is lacking, I recoil and give up at the slightest resistance. I know the way of perfection and see clearly enough how I ought to act, but because I am pressed down by the weight of my own corruption I do not rise to more perfect things.

How extremely necessary to me, O Lord, your grace is to begin any good deed, to carry it on and bring it to completion! For without grace I can do nothing, but with its strength I can do all things in you. O Grace truly heavenly, without which our merits are nothing and no gifts of nature are to be esteemed!

Before you, O Lord, no arts or riches, no beauty or strength, no wit or intelligence avail without grace. For the gifts of nature are common to good and bad alike, but your special gift is grace or love, and those who are signed with it are held worthy of everlasting life. So excellent is this grace that without it no gift of prophecy or of miracles, no meditation be it ever so exalted, can be considered anything. Not even faith or hope or other virtues are acceptable to you without love and grace.

O most blessed Grace, which makes the poor in spirit rich in virtues, which renders one who is rich in many good things humble of heart, come, descend upon me, fill me quickly with your consolation before my soul faints with weariness and mental dryness.

Let me find grace in your sight, I beg, Lord, for your grace is enough for me, even though I obtain none of the things that nature desires. If I am tempted and afflicted with many tribulations, I will fear no evils while your grace is with me. This is my strength. This will give me counsel and help. This is more powerful than all my enemies and wiser than all the wise. This is the mistress of truth, the teacher of discipline, the light of the heart. It consoles in anguish, banishes sorrow, expels fear, nourishes devotion, and produces tears. What am I without grace, but dead wood, a useless branch, fit only to be cast away?

Let your grace, therefore, go before me and follow me, O Lord, and make me always intent upon good works, through Jesus Christ, your Son.

fOLLOWING JESUS

From Book III, Chapter 56

This short chapter offers a summary of the first three books.

CHRIST: My child, the more you depart from yourself, the more you will be able to enter into me. As the giving up of exterior things brings interior peace, so the forsaking of self unites you to God. I want you to learn perfect surrender to my will, without contradiction or complaint.

Follow me. *I am the way, and the truth, and the life.* Without the way, there is no going. Without the truth, there is no knowing. Without the life, there is no living. I am the way that you must follow, the truth that you must believe, the life for which you must hope. I am the inviolable way, the infallible truth, the unending life. I am the way that is straight, the supreme truth, the life that is true, the blessed, the uncreated life. If you abide in my way, *you will know the truth, and the truth will make you free,* and you will attain life everlasting.

If you wish to enter into life, keep the commandments. If you wish to know the truth, believe in me. *If you wish to be perfect, sell your possessions.* If you wish to be my disciple, deny yourself. If you wish to possess the blessed life, despise this present life. If you wish to be exalted in heaven, humble yourself on earth. If you wish to reign with me, carry the cross with me.

appendix

Reading Spiritual Classics for Personal and Group Formation

Many Christians today are searching for more spiritual depth, for something more than simply being good church members. That quest may send them to the spiritual practices of New Age movements or of Eastern religions such as Zen Buddhism. Christians, though, have their own long spiritual tradition, a tradition rich with wisdom, variety, and depth.

The great spiritual classics testify to that depth. They do not concern themselves with mystical flights for a spiritual elite. Rather, they contain very practical advice and insights that can support and shape the spiritual growth of any Christian. We can all benefit by sitting at the feet of the masters (both male and female) of Christian spirituality.

Reading spiritual classics is different from most of the reading we do. We have learned to read to master a text and extract information from it. We tend to read quickly, to get through a text. And we summarize as we read, seeking the main point. In reading spiritual classics, though, we allow the text to master and form us. Such formative reading goes more slowly, more reflectively, allowing time for God to speak to us through the text. God's word for us may come as easily from a minor point or even an aside as from the major point.

Formative reading requires that you approach the text in humility. Read as a seeker, not an expert. Don't demand that the text meet your expectations for what an "enlightened" author should write. Humility means accepting the author as another imperfect human, a product of his or her own time and situation. Learn to celebrate what is foundational in an author's writing without being overly disturbed by what is peculiar to the author's life and times. Trust the text as a gift from both God and the author, offered to you for your benefit—to help you grow in Christ.

To read formatively, you must also slow down. Feel free to reread a passage that seems to speak specially to you. Stop from time to time to reflect on what you have been reading. Keep a journal for these reflections. Often the act of writing can itself prompt further, deeper reflection. Keep your notebook open and your pencil in hand as you read. You might not get back to that wonderful insight later. Don't worry that you are not getting through an entire passage—or even the first paragraph! Formative reading is about depth rather than breadth, quality rather than quantity. As you read, seek God's direction for your own life. Timeless truths have their place but may not be what is most important for your own formation here and now.

As you read the passage, you might keep some of these questions running through your mind:

- How is what I'm reading true of my own life? Where does it reflect my own *experience*?

- How does this text challenge me? What new *direction* does it offer me?

- What must I change to put what I am reading into practice? How can I *incarnate* it, let this word become flesh in my life?

You might also devote special attention to sections that upset you. What is the source of the disturbance? Do you want to argue theology? Are you turned off by cultural differences? Or have you been skewered by an insight that would turn your life upside down if you took it seriously? Let your journal be a dialogue with the text.

If you find yourself moving from reading the text to chewing over its implications to praying, that's great! Spiritual reading is really the first step in an ancient way of prayer called *lectio divina* or "divine reading." Reading leads naturally into reflection on what you have read (meditation). As you reflect on what the text might mean for your life, you may well want to ask for God's help in living out any new insights or direction you have perceived (prayer). Sometimes such prayer may lead you further into silently abiding in God's presence (contemplation). And, of course, the process is only really completed when it begins to make a difference in the way we live (incarnation).

As good as it is to read spiritual classics in solitude, it is even better to join with others in a small group for mutual formation or "spiritual direction in common." This is *not* the same as a study group that talks about spiritual classics. A group for mutual formation would have similar goals as for an individual's reading: to allow the text to shine its light on the *experiences* of the group members, to suggest new *directions* for their lives and practical ways of *incarnating* these directions. Such a group might agree to focus on one short passage from a classic at each meeting (even if members have read more). Discussion usually goes much deeper if all the members have already read and reflected on the passage before the meeting and bring their journals.

Such groups need to watch for several potential problems. It is easy to go off on a tangent (especially if it takes the focus off the members' own experience and onto generalities). At such times a group leader might bring the group's attention back to the text: "What does our author say about that?" Or, "How do we experience that in our own lives?" When a group member shares a problem, others may be tempted to try to "fix" it. This is much less helpful than sharing similar experiences and how they were handled (for good or ill). "Sharing" someone else's problems (whether that person is in or out of the group) should be strongly discouraged.

One person could be designated as leader, to be responsible for opening and closing prayers; to be the first to share or respond to the text; and to keep notes during the discussion to highlight recurring themes, challenges, directives, or practical steps. These responsibilities could also be shared among several members of the group or rotated.

For further information about formative reading of spiritual classics, try *A Practical Guide to Spiritual Reading* by Susan Annette Muto. *Shaped by the Word* by Robert Mulholland (Upper Room Books) covers formative reading of the Bible. *Good Things Happen: Experiencing Community in Small Groups* by Dick Westley is an excellent resource on forming small groups of all kinds.